PLANFT EART

ROCKS AND FOSSILS

By Jim Pipe

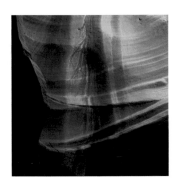

Copyright © ticktock Entertainment Ltd 2008

First published in Great Britain in 2008 by ticktock Media Ltd,
2 Orchard Business Centre, North Farm Road, Tunbridge Wells, Kent, TN2 3XF

ticktock project editor: Ruth Owen
ticktock picture researcher: Lizzie Knowles
ticktock project designer: Emma Randall
With thanks to: Terry Jennings, Jean Coppendale, Suzy Gazlay and Elizabeth Wiggans

ISBN 978 1 84696 520 3 pbk
Printed in China

A CIP catalogue record for this book is available from the British Library.

Picture credits (t=top; b=bottom; c=centre; l=left; r=right):
Alamy: 15rt, 18ct. Corbis royalty free: 16lb. istock: 6lc. Layne Kennedy/ Corbis: 25tl. NASA: 29rb. Natural History Museum: 22c.
Rex Features: 19cb, 21 main. Shutterstock: OFC all, 1 all, 3, 4lt, 4lc, 4lb, 4cb, 4–5 main, 5rt, 5rc, 5rb, 6l (top 3), 6l (diamond ring),
6 main, 7rc, 8lt, 8lb, 8–9 main, 10lt, 10–11 main, 11rt, 11rb, 12l all, 12–13 main, 13rt, 13rb, 14lt, 14–15 main, 15b, 15rc, 15rb,
17b all, 18lt, 18lc, 18lb, 18 main, 19rt, 19rc, 19rb, 20lt, 20lc, 20rt, 20rc, 21rt, 21rc, 21rb, 22b, 26b, 27 main, 28lt, 30–31 all, OBC
all. Science Photo Library: 7c, 7rb, 11rc, 16lc, 16 main, 23 main, 24 main, 28 main, 29 main,29rc. Superstock: 4l, 6lb, 10lb,13b,
16lt, 27rt. ticktock Media Ltd: 7rt, 8lc, 9rt, 9rb, 13rc, 17t, 22l all, 23r all, 24lc, 24lb, 25b, 25rt, 25rc, 25rb, 26l all.

CONTENTS

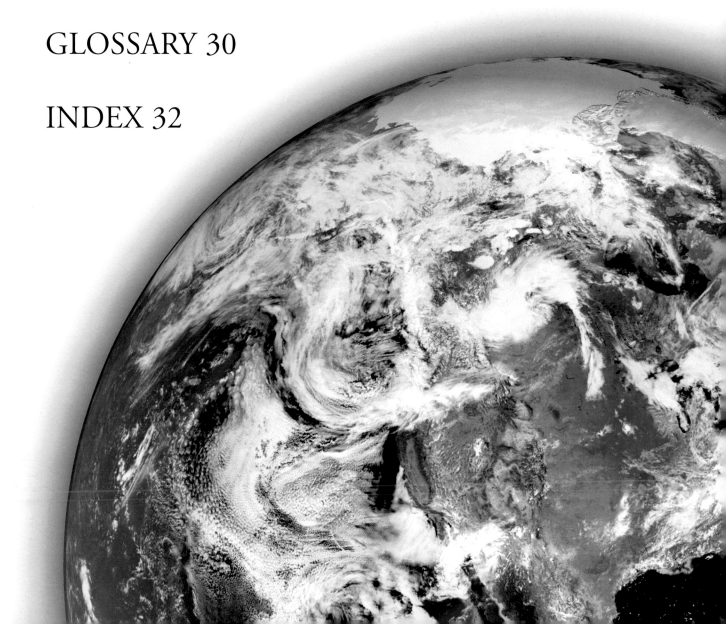

CHAPTER 1:
Our Rocky Planet

Have you ever watched an excavator dig a deep hole in the ground? If it keeps digging down, it will always hit solid rock sooner or later. That's because our Earth is a giant ball of rock.

ROCKS ARE EVERYWHERE

Layers of rock cover the entire surface of our planet. This rocky outer layer of our planet is called the crust. In places where there are landmasses, the Earth's crust is up to 40 kilometres thick.

You can find rocks everywhere, from mountains and riverbanks to beaches and caves.

Layers of rock are hidden under soil, water or ice.

If you were climbing up a cliff face, you would be face to face with the Earth's crust.

You cannot see the rocks below our cities, but they are there!

THE HIDDEN CRUST

Oceans cover over 70 percent of the Earth's crust. Below the oceans, the crust is thinner than where there are landmasses. In places it is only seven kilometres thick. However, if you went to the bottom of the ocean, you would see mountains and valleys just like those on land. The Earth's rocky crust is also hidden at the South Pole. It is underneath a three kilometre-thick layer of ice.

In some parts of the Earth's crust, the rocks are really ancient. Rocks have been found in Greenland that are over four billion years old. However, new rocks are forming all the time – right below your feet!

THE EARTH'S ROCKS

There are three main types of rocks on Earth – igneous rocks, sedimentary rocks and metamorphic rocks. They are all formed in different ways.

This photograph shows Cedar Breaks National Monument in Utah, USA. This vast, bowl-shaped limestone cliff extends 600 metres downwards. You can see the different colours and layers of rock that make up the Earth's crust.

MAKING ROCKS

IGNEOUS ROCKS

Igneous rocks are rocks that harden from molten magma or lava. Some igneous rocks form from magma deep inside the Earth. Others form on the Earth's surface. Lava from volcanoes cools and hardens to form igneous rocks. Granite is a type of igneous rock. The giant faces of four American presidents are carved in granite at Mount Rushmore in South Dakota, USA.

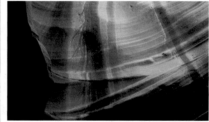

SEDIMENTARY ROCKS

Sedimentary rocks are formed from layers of sediment (grains of rock). Over many years, pressure from the layers above and low heat packs the sediments together. Eventually the layers join up and form rocks. You can usually see the layers of sediment in sedimentary rocks. Sandstone is a type of sedimentary rock.

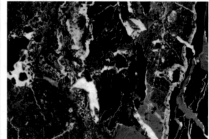

METAMORPHIC ROCKS

Metamorphic rocks are rocks that have been transformed from one type of rock into another. This happens deep underground. Most metamorphic rocks form because of great heat and pressure deep within the Earth. Marble is a type of metamorphic rock.

GEMSTONES

Some rare and beautiful minerals are known as gemstones. They are rough when first taken out of the ground, but they sparkle when they have been cut into shapes and polished. Each of these minerals has its own unique shape and colour.

A POLISHED SAPPHIRE

AMETHYST CRYSTALS

A RAW OPAL

A POLISHED EMERALD SET IN A RING

A POLISHED DIAMOND SET IN A RING

A RUBY AND DIAMOND BROOCH

WHAT ARE ROCKS MADE FROM?

Rocks are made from substances called minerals. These are solid chemicals which are found in nature. Minerals are inorganic. This means they do not come from plants or animals. However, plants and animals do need certain minerals to survive. You need the calcium in milk for healthy bones. One mineral you probably eat every day is salt. Common table salt is made from the mineral halite.

WHAT ARE MINERALS?

You probably know more minerals that you realise. Gold, silver and the gemstones used in jewellery are all minerals. You can also find minerals in everyday objects, such as the graphite, or lead, in pencils.

About 3,800 minerals have been found on Earth, but most are rare. Every type of rock has its own unique combination of one or more minerals. For example, pure sandstone is made from just one mineral – quartz. Quartz is one of the most common minerals. Granite is mainly made up of three minerals – feldspar, quartz and mica.

Like this piece of quartz, a specific mineral always has the same makeup. Each mineral has a definite shape.

WHAT ARE CRYSTALS?

In nature, minerals usually occur in geometrical shapes called crystals. They have smooth faces, straight edges and symmetrical corners. Halite (table salt) crystals are shaped like tiny cubes. Zircon crystals are shaped like a pyramid. They are often used in jewellery. Millions of tiny crystals often cluster together to make a chunk of rock. Most gemstones are crystals.

These table salt crystals have been magnified using a scanning electron microscope. They are the salt crystals you sprinkle on your food.

GROW YOUR OWN CRYSTALS

Materials needed
- 200g of white alum or Epsom salts (from a chemist or supermarket)
- ½ litre of water
- Saucepan
- Bowl
- Spoon
- Jar with lid
- Tissue paper
- Magnifying glass

1) Pour the water into a pan. Then add about 200 grams of alum. Ask an adult to heat the water, stirring it until the alum dissolves. Don't let the water boil.

2) Pour half the solution into a bowl and half into a clean jar. Cover the jar to keep out the dust.

3) After a few days, small crystals will appear in the bowl. When they are about 3 to 4 millimetres across, pour away the solution and dry the crystals.

4) Pour the fresh solution from the jar into the bowl. Put one of the best crystals into the solution.

5) After a few days, the crystal will have grown even bigger. Remove it and dry it with tissue paper. Then look at the crystal through a magnifying glass.

Crystals grow into weird and wonderful shapes. Some are like needles. Others look like kidneys or tree trunks. What shape are your crystals?

INSIDE THE EARTH

MAGMA
The magma that makes up the Earth's mantle is super hot. It can reach temperatures of up to 4,150°C.

CRUST

MANTLE

OUTER CORE

CORE

The edges of the Earth's tectonic plates are shown in red on this map. The plates fit together like a jigsaw puzzle.

VOLCANOES

Volcanoes are found on the boundary between two tectonic plates. Red-hot magma is pushed to the surface from deep in the mantle. When magma reaches the surface it is called lava. It flows out of the volcano, mixed with gas and steam. Fresh lava has a temperature of 700 to 1,200 °C. Sometimes volcanoes erupt violently. They can blow out lava, rocks, ash and clouds of steam at speeds of over 500 km/h.

CHAPTER 2:
How Rocks Are Formed

Around 4.3 billion years ago, the Earth was a giant ball of molten, or liquid, red-hot rock. Over millions of years, the surface of the planet cooled and became the solid, rocky crust.

BENEATH THE EARTH'S CRUST

Beneath the Earth's crust lies a layer of incredibly hot rock called the mantle. The mantle is solid near the surface. But deeper down, the mantle flows like melted tar. The crust floats on top of the mantle. The Earth's crust and the solid upper section of the mantle are known as the lithosphere.

EARTH'S TECTONIC PLATES

The lithosphere is broken into huge pieces, called tectonic plates. The tectonic plates support the continents and oceans. They are constantly moving, but don't worry – the movements are usually very, very slow. However, over a long time, this movement creates big changes on the Earth's surface.

CRUST AND MOUNTAIN-BUILDING

When two plates move apart, hot liquid magma from the mantle pushes up to fill the gap. This creates new crust material. Iceland, in the North Atlantic Ocean, was created in this way. When two plates crash into each other, they crumple and push giant chunks of rock upwards to form mountains.

Some mountains are formed by volcanic activity. After a volcanic eruption, the lava cools and hardens on the surface. Each time the volcano erupts, the mountain grows larger. Mount Fuji in Japan formed this way.

MAKING MOUNTAINS

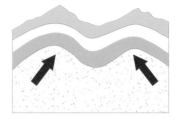

FOLD MOUNTAINS
Sometimes tectonic plate movements can force rocks to push against each other, fold and rise up.

THE ANDES
The Andes are the world's longest chain of mountains. They run down the west coast of South America for around 8,800 kilometres. The Andes are fold mountains. They were formed when an ocean plate crashed into a continental plate about 70 million years ago.

THE HIMALAYAS
The Himalayas is the highest mountain range in the world. The Himalayas are also fold mountains. About 50 million years ago, the tectonic plate carrying India bumped into the plate carrying China. The plates crumpled, pushing rock upwards.

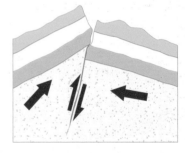

FAULT MOUNTAINS
Sometimes the Earth's surface cracks. The crack is called a fault. Layers of rock on one side of the fault can be pushed up to form a mountain or mountain range.

Basalt is a type of extrusive igneous rock. When basalt hardens it can form regular hexagonal shapes. These shapes can be seen at the famous Giant's Causeway in County Antrim, Northern Ireland.

IGNEOUS ROCKS

As well as creating mountains, volcanoes help to bring new rocks to the Earth's surface. When hot lava comes to the surface, it cools and forms hard igneous rocks. Igneous means 'fiery' – just like the magma these rocks are made from.

Different types of igneous rock are formed depending on how quickly the magma or lava cools. On the surface, lava cools quickly.

PLUTONS

Magma escapes through openings in the Earth's crust. Magma can also gather in reservoirs under the ground. Sometimes a molten magma reservoir hardens into a giant lump of underground rock. This giant lump of rock is called a pluton. Some plutons are hundreds of kilometres wide. On Dartmoor in southwest England, you can see granite rock formations called tors (below). The tors are the remains of plutons that were once underground. They were revealed when the softer rock above them wore away.

It forms extrusive rocks such as basalt. The crystals in basalt are small because they formed quickly.

Sometimes, magma does not make it to the surface. It is forced into cracks underground. Here it cools slowly. It forms intrusive rocks such as granite. The crystals in granite are larger. This is because the magma cooled slowly and the crystals took longer to form.

These are the granite mountains in Yosemite National Park, USA. They were once huge underground domes of intrusive magma. The softer rocks around them have been worn away over millions of years.

EXAMPLES OF IGNEOUS ROCKS

PUMICE

Pumice is the only rock that can float. It has air bubbles trapped inside it. A pumice stone (above) can be rubbed on your hands to clean them. Tiny bits of pumice are also used in facial and body scrubs.

OBSIDIAN

When red-hot lava flows into the sea, it cools very quickly. This produces a glassy rock called obsidian. This natural volcanic glass has a razor-sharp edge. Ancient people once made spear and axe heads using obsidian. It is also shiny enough to use as a mirror.

TUFF

These giant statues stand guard over Easter Island, in the Pacific Ocean. They are known as moai. The statues were carved from a type of volcanic rock called tuff. Some moai are 4.5 metres tall and weigh 80 tonnes!

The Rocky Mountains (above) formed about 70 to 40 million years ago. The Appalachian Mountains (below) formed about 480 million years ago. Weathering has smoothed out their shape over time.

WEATHERING

Look at the picture of the Rocky Mountains in North America (above left). They look tall and jagged. Now look at the Appalachian Mountains (below left). These mountains are more rounded and much lower. That's because over millions of years, wind, water, ice and the Sun's heat have worn them away. This is called weathering.

SAND, CLAY AND SILT

Large areas of bare rock are the quickest to wear away. This is because they don't get any protection from plants and soil. When rocks break down into smaller and smaller pieces, they turn into sand, clay or silt. If you looked at sand under a microscope, you would see that it is made up of the same minerals as the rocks it came from.

Over the last million years, the Colorado River in Arizona, USA, has been changing the land around it. The river has a cut a gorge up to 1.8 kilometres deep through the Earth's crust. This gorge is the Grand Canyon!

WATER AT WORK

Waves pounding against a cliff can cause a cave to form. In time, the cave becomes an arch (above). This arch eventually collapses, leaving a sea stack (below).

WATER POWER

Water causes weathering, too. Waves fling pebbles against cliffs. Rocks and pebbles rub against each other in rough water. This wears the rocks down into shingle and sand. Rushing water also cuts into rock. The sand and stones carried by a river also wear away at riverbanks.

SHATTERING ROCKS

Mountain rocks are often shattered by ice. When water trickles into the crack in a rock, it can freeze. As it turns to ice, the water expands and makes the crack bigger. When the ice melts, more water trickles into the crack. This water will then freeze, too. Each time water in the crack freezes, the crack will get bigger. Eventually, the rock breaks along the crack.

SOIL

When tiny pieces of rock mix with the remains of dead plants and animals, soil is created. Different types of rocks create different types of soil. The process of creating soil is speeded up by plant roots. As trees and other plants grow, their roots work into cracks, splitting rocks apart. This plant activity, and animals burrowing in soil, helps to break up new soil into smaller and smaller pieces.

HOW ICE BREAKS ROCKS

Materials needed
- Piece of old brick (the type used for housebuilding)
- Or, a piece of blackboard chalk
- A bowl of water
- A plastic bag

1) Put the piece of brick or chalk into a bowl of water. Let it soak for 4 to 5 hours.
2) Put the brick or chalk into the plastic bag. Place the bag in the freezer overnight.

Don't forget brick!

3) Observe what has happened the following morning. (Depending on how porous the brick is, it might need longer in the freezer.)

When the water inside the brick or piece of chalk freezes, it will expand. This breaks the brick or chalk into pieces.

Conglomerate is a coarse rock. It is often formed in areas where there is lots of moving water, such as beaches. It can be made up of pebbles and even boulders.

EROSION

The broken bits of rock created by weathering are washed away by streams and rivers. Sometimes they are blown away by the wind. This is called erosion. Eventually this material is swept down to lakes or the ocean. It gathers on the bottom of lakes and oceans with sea shells and other minerals. This mixture of fragments of rock and other material is called sediment. Over thousands of years, layers of sediment build up.

SEDIMENTARY ROCKS

One layer of sediment is not very thick. But think of a telephone directory. All the thin sheets of paper add up to a heavy weight. Layers of sediment create a heavy weight, too. They crush and put pressure on the layers below them. Slowly, over millions of years, the sediments turn into rocks. These are called sedimentary rocks. Large sediments create conglomerates, or puddingstone. These rocks are made up of pebbles that have become glued together by sand that has turned to solid stone. Medium-sized sediments create sandstone. Fine sediments turn to clay. Many rocks you will see in your daily life are sedimentary rocks, such as chalk, sandstone and limestone.

FLICKING THROUGH HISTORY

Sedimentary rocks are made up of layers formed over millions of years. They can provide a very good record of the past. Cutting through layers of sedimentary rock is like flicking through the pages of Earth's history – a history that is billions of years old! Sedimentary rocks often contain fossils of plants, animals, and microbes. Coal is a sedimentary rock formed from the remains of ancient forests.

The Vermillion Cliffs in Utah, USA, are made of sandstone. Weathering and erosion has created many unusual shapes, such as these 'tee-pees'. The sand was deposited millions of years ago as huge sand dunes. The swirling patterns in the layers of sediment were made by the wind.

EXAMPLES OF SEDIMENTARY ROCKS

TIGER EYE
Ironstone is a sedimentary rock. It sometimes contains bands of yellow quartz. This is known as 'tiger eye' because of its yellow and brown stripes. Roman soldiers are said to have worn polished lumps of tiger eye. They believed it would ward off evil in battle.

SANDSTONE
Sandstone is used a lot as a building material. It occurs in many different colours, such as brown, yellow, red, grey and white. It has been used here to build the Palace of Winds in Jaipur, India.

CLAY
Not all rocks are hard. The soft clay used to make pots is a type of rock. You can tell what minerals are in clay from the colour. Grey clay contains carbon. Red clay contains iron oxides.

STALACTITES AND STALAGMITES
Rainwater can slowly dissolve limestone rock. When this water drips from the roof of a cave, some of it evaporates. It leaves behind a deposit of limestone. Over hundreds of years, the limestone builds up to form a rock 'icicle' or stalactite. When water drops hit the floor of a cave, they also leave tiny deposits. These slowly build up into the columns known as stalagmites.

MARBLE
Marble is a beautiful metamorphic rock often used in building and sculpture. The Italian artist Michelangelo used marble for his famous statue of David.

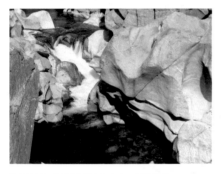

GNEISS (PRONOUNCED 'NICE')
Gneiss is created by a combination of heat and pressure on the igneous rock, granite. The gneiss rocks (above) are on the Verzasca River in Switzerland. They were raised to the surface as the Alps were formed. They have been weathered and eroded by the river and weather.

TRINITITE
In July 1945, the world's first atomic bomb was tested in the Muerto Desert in New Mexico. The heat and pressure melted the sandy desert ground. The sand became a shiny green metamorphic rock, called trinitite.

BAKED AND SQUEEZED

Rocks are formed from magma and lava, and from layers of sediment. There is also a third way that new rocks are created. Metamorphic rocks can be formed from igneous, sedimentary or other metamorphic rocks. This happens deep underground. Most metamorphic rocks form because of great heat and pressure deep within the Earth. The texture, appearance and chemical composition of the rock can be changed by the heat from magma. It's rather like the way a cake changes when you bake it. Rocks can also be changed from one type to another by the enormous pressures and heat caused by two tectonic plates bumping into each other.

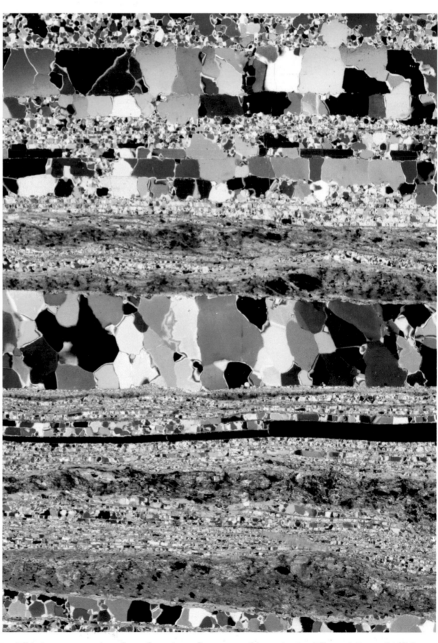

This is a cross-section through a piece of metamorphic mylonite. The rock is made of the minerals mica (the grey, darker sections) and quartz (the coloured sections).

METAMORPHIC ROCKS

Rocks that have been changed by heat and pressure under the ground are called metamorphic rocks. Metamorphic means 'change of form'. These rocks often have swirling patterns. This is because the rock partly melts as it forms. Some metamorphic rocks, such as marble, are created by heat alone. A few, such as mylonite, are created just by pressure.

THE ROCK CYCLE

The rock cycle is a constant process of change.
The rock cycle changes rocks from one type into another.
It is happening around us and under our feet all the time!

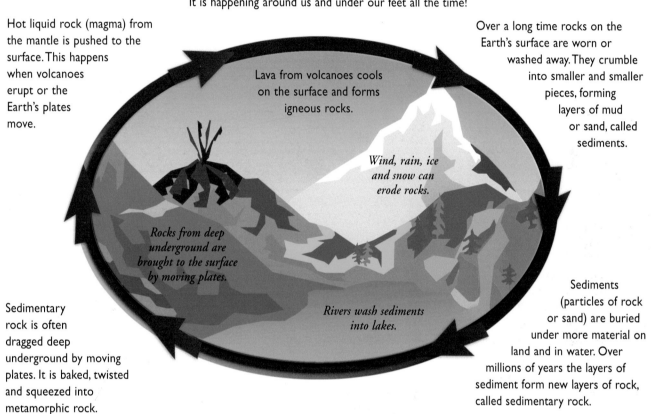

Hot liquid rock (magma) from the mantle is pushed to the surface. This happens when volcanoes erupt or the Earth's plates move.

Over a long time rocks on the Earth's surface are worn or washed away. They crumble into smaller and smaller pieces, forming layers of mud or sand, called sediments.

Lava from volcanoes cools on the surface and forms igneous rocks.

Wind, rain, ice and snow can erode rocks.

Rocks from deep underground are brought to the surface by moving plates.

Sedimentary rock is often dragged deep underground by moving plates. It is baked, twisted and squeezed into metamorphic rock.

Rivers wash sediments into lakes.

Sediments (particles of rock or sand) are buried under more material on land and in water. Over millions of years the layers of sediment form new layers of rock, called sedimentary rock.

ALL CHANGE

The original rock that is changed into metamorphic rock is known as parent rock. Some rocks change several times. Under low heat and pressure, the sedimentary rock shale turns into slate. But as it gets squeezed and baked further, slate then changes into phyllite. Finally phyllite can change into schist.

SHALE	SLATE	PHYLLITE	SCHIST

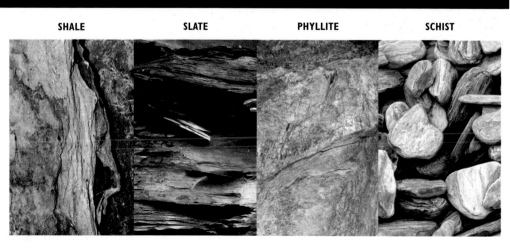

ULURU

Uluru is a huge rock in Uluru-Kata Tjuta National Park in central Australia. It is one of the world's largest single pieces of rock. Uluru is 348 metres high. It is about 2 kilometres long and extends 2.5 kilometres into the ground. It is a sacred site for Australian Aboriginal people.

SHIPROCK PINNACLE

The Shiprock Pinnacle in New Mexico, USA, rises 550 metres above the surrounding plain. It is all that is left of an ancient volcano. The rock is the solidified lava core of the volcano.

SUGAR LOAF MOUNTAIN

The enormous dome-shaped Sugar Loaf Mountain towers above the Brazilian city of Rio de Janeiro. The granite peak is around 395 metres high. It is part of a small chain of mountains.

CHAPTER 3: Rocks At Work

People have been using rocks for thousands of years. Common rocks such as sandstone, granite, slate and limestone are used to build houses and public buildings. Marble is carved into statues, pillars or tiles to decorate those buildings.

MODERN BUILDING MATERIALS

One of our most useful building materials today is concrete. It is made from crushed rocks and gravel mixed with cement and sand. Cement is made from a mix of clay and powdered limestone. Clay is also used to make bricks. It is baked in a kiln (a large oven) to make it harder and stronger.

Slate is a metamorphic rock that can be split easily into thin sheets. It makes a good roofing material. It is also used to make floor tiles.

Pure sand is made almost entirely from the mineral silica. When pure sand is heated, it can be made into glass.

QUARRIES

Quarrying is cutting large blocks of rock from a hole on the Earth's surface or from a cliff face. This can be difficult. Explosives are often used to blast rocks out of cliff faces in a quarry. Explosives are also used to break the chunks of rock into smaller pieces.

Powerful machines drill a line of holes into the ground at a quarry. The holes are then packed with explosives. The explosives are detonated (set off) from a safe distance.

PREHISTORIC USES FOR ROCK

The first mines were dug by early humans about 10,000 years ago. These prehistoric miners used small pits and tunnels to find flint. By chipping away at a rock edge, they could make flint into sharp tools and weapons. Early humans also found that when wet clay dried, it turned hard. This was how the first pottery was created. Cave paintings in France were made on rocks over 17,000 years ago. The paints were made from crushed up rocks and minerals.

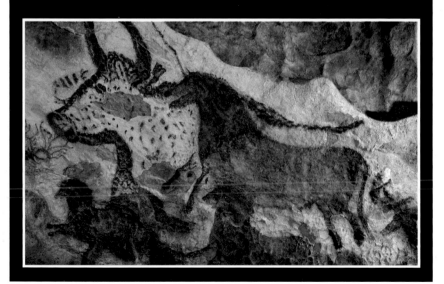

ROCKS IN HISTORY

ROCK CITY

At Petra in Jordan, a city was carved into the banded sandstone rock over 2,000 years ago.

STONEHENGE

The famous stone circle of Stonehenge in Wiltshire was built in stages between 3,100 and 1,500 BC. Some of the stone pillars weigh up to 50 tonnes each. They are made from a hard sandstone known as sarsen.

THE TAJ MAHAL

The Taj Mahal in India was built in the mid 1600s by the Emperor Shah Jahan. This magnificent white marble building was built in memory of the Shah's wife. Marble is a favourite among sculptors because of its gleaming colour that changes with the light. Its fine grain makes it easy to work with.

Talc is a soft mineral. It is used to make talcum powder, paint and crayons.

USEFUL MINERALS

Rocks are also quarried and mined for the minerals they contain. These minerals provide the raw materials for almost all the appliances in our homes, from TV sets to microwave ovens.

The silicon chips inside computers are made from the mineral silica. The mineral sulphur is used to make explosives, sulphuric acid, dyes, matches, rubber, insecticides and medicines. Farmers spray their crops with fertilisers that contain minerals such as nitrates and potash.

Quartz crystals create an electric charge when they are squeezed. They are fitted into clocks and watches to help them keep time.

Gold is used on the visors of astronauts' helmets. The gold protects the astronauts against harmful rays from the Sun.

Copper ore was first mined about 10,000 years ago. It was used to make weapons and jewellery. Today, it is used to make electric wires and water pipes.

IDENTIFYING MINERALS

No two minerals are exactly the same. Every mineral has a mix of features that make it unique. Hardness is measured on a scale devised by German geologist Friedrich Mohs. On Mohs' scale, one is the softest mineral, while 10 is the hardest.

FEATURE	DIAMOND	CRYSTAL QUARTZ	GRAPHITE
CLEAVAGE How a mineral breaks	When struck can break in four directions	No specific way	Breaks perfectly in one direction
STREAK The colour of the mineral if you crush it into powder	White	White	Grey-black
HARDNESS How easily does it scratch?	10 Mohs (maximum)	7 Mohs	1-2 Mohs (1 is minimum)
LUSTRE Is it shiny?	Very shiny	Glassy	Shiny when wet
TRANSPARENCY How easy is it to see through?	Transparent	Translucent	Opaque
COLOUR Some minerals have several colours	Clear	White, purple, yellow, green and blue	Dark grey or black

Miners use a drill to remove gold from a mine in South Africa.

ORES

Pure gold, silver, iron, tin and copper are all mined from rocks in the ground, called ores. The ore that contains gold is often found in hard rock deep underground. It is removed by drills and cutting machines. In some places gold appears as a thin streak, or vein, running through rock. Pure gold can also appear as large lumps, called nuggets.

DIAMONDS ARE FOREVER

Diamonds are the hardest materials on Earth. Drills that have diamonds on their tips can cut through any other material. Incredible heat and pressure turns the element carbon into diamonds. This happens at least 150 kilometres below the Earth's surface. Diamonds are brought close to the surface by volcanic eruptions.

TESTING MINERALS

Materials needed
- Selection of different minerals
- Ceramic kitchen or bathroom tile
- Safety goggle
- Small hammer
- Torch

1) POWDER COLOUR

Carefully scratch a mark across the back of a ceramic tile with any mineral. The scratch, or streak, will be the colour of the mineral's powder.

2) TRANSPARENCY

Test a mineral's transparency by shining a torch through it. How easily can you see through the mineral?

3) CLEAVAGE

Hit a mineral sample with a small hammer – don't try this on expensive gems and ALWAYS wear safety goggles! Some minerals break leaving rough and uneven surfaces. Other minerals break cleanly in one or more directions, leaving a flat, even surface.

4) HARDNESS

Hardness is measured in Mohs but you can guess a mineral's hardness using everyday objects. If you can scratch a mineral with a fingernail it has a hardness less than 2.5 Mohs. If it takes a knife to scratch it, the mineral has a hardness around 5.5 Mohs.

CHAPTER 4:
Fossils

Many of the rocks under your feet are millions or even billions of years old. By looking at layers of rock, we can study Earth's history. One of the best ways to do this is to look at fossils.

When some ancient plants and animals died, they were buried under layers of sand and mud. Over time, more and more layers of mud or sand covered the remains.

The weight of the ground above the remains put huge pressure on them. They hardened into solid rock. Minerals replaced the organic matter of the bones until they became rock-like copies of the bones – fossils!

Fossils are the rocky remains of animals and plants that were alive millions of years ago. Almost all fossils are found in sedimentary rock. This type of rock is formed from sediments found in swamps, lakes and oceans. Many fossils are of sea animals or animals that lived near water. Scientists have discovered fossils of fish, birds, insects, shrimps and flowers. They have also found fossils of giant dinosaurs.

Some fossils are actually powering our cars and heating our homes. Fossils formed from plants and microscopic animals turned into fossil fuels, such as coal, gas and oil.

In Montana, USA, 40 fossilised dinosaur nests and eggs were found. They belonged to the plant-eating dinosaur, Maiasaura. They showed that these dinosaurs laid their eggs in a big group, just like many birds do today. This image is a museum reconstruction of a Maiasaura nest.

Fossils are pushed to the surface by movements in the Earth's crust. They can also appear after wind or water has worn away the rock around them.

WHAT GETS FOSSILISED?

Fossils aren't just bones. They can be the remains of teeth, shells and plants. In a few rare cases even the squishy bits from inside an animal have been found. In the 1990s, a Thescelosaurus skeleton was found in South Dakota, USA. It had a fossilised heart. Sometimes ancient insects became trapped in resin, the sticky liquid that oozes from pine trees. Over millions of years, this hardened to become the yellow gemstone amber. The insects were trapped inside.

MAKING FOSSILS

Materials needed
- Shells or tough leaves with prominent veins
- Lump of modelling clay
- Rolling pin
- Cooking oil
- Plaster of Paris
- Water

1) Roll out the lump of clay until it is flat and smooth. Press an object such as a shell or leaf into the clay.

2) Pull the object out of the clay.

In real life, bacteria usually makes the body part or leaf rot away.

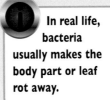

3) Rub a small amount of cooking oil on to the impression to make a non-stick surface. Then make some plaster of Paris in a ratio of two parts plaster to one part water.

4) Quickly spoon at least one centimetre of plaster into the impression made by the object.

In real life, minerals in underground water fill the space left by the rotting body parts or leaf. This takes millions of years.

5) Leave the plaster to completely dry overnight. Peel away the clay. You now have a cast of the original object.

 This is exactly what happens in nature. A fossil is a cast of the original animal or plant.

This rock contains fossils of crinoids, or sea lillies. These marine creatures lived about 440 to 360 million years ago. Crinoids attached themselves to the seabed using their stalks. They captured food using their feathery arms.

FOSSIL HISTORY OF THE EARTH

The history of the Earth is broken down into a series of eras and then periods. Each period has its own range of fossils. This fossil timeline gives us a guide for dating rocks.

PALAEOZOIC ERA

PRECAMBRIAN PERIOD
Before 540 million years ago
Simple plants and animals evolve.

CAMBRIAN PERIOD
540 to 500 million years ago
First animals with skeletons appear.

Ammonite

ORDOVICIAN PERIOD
500 to 435 million years ago
Primitive fish, and prehistoric shellfish, such as trilobites and ammonites, evolve.

SILURIAN PERIOD
435 to 410 million years ago
Fish with jaws develop and land creatures appear.

Cephalaspis

DEVONIAN PERIOD
410 to 355 million years ago
Trees and insects appear. Seas filled with bony fish, such as *Cephalaspis*.

CARBONIFEROUS PERIOD
355 to 295 million years ago
The first forests grow and the first reptiles appear.

PERMIAN PERIOD
295 to 251 million years ago
Conifer trees and sail-backed reptiles appear.

THE TIMELINE IS CONTINUED ON PAGE 25

DINOSAUR HUNTING

Would you like to track down a dinosaur? You will need to find some sedimentary rock from the right period. To find *Tyrannosaurus rex* fossils, you'll need to track down rocks that were formed during the late Cretaceous Period. Areas where rocks wear away quickly because of rain or wind are a good place to look for fossils.

EXCAVATING FOSSILS

Getting fossils out of the ground is hard work. Picks can remove large chunks of rock. The last few centimetres of rock are then chipped away with small hand tools. A quick-setting glue is sprayed on fossils to stop them breaking. Then they are wrapped in layers of plaster and taken to a laboratory.

TRACE FOSSILS

Fossil hunters also look for trace fossils. These are marks made by animals, such as footprints, burrows, eggs and dung. A footprint can show what the surface of a dinosaur's skin was like. Fossilised tracks can show whether an animal was part of a group. Tracks also show if an animal dragged its tail or even if it had a limp.

Coprolites are dinosaur dung fossils – though the smell is long gone! Some scientists spend their whole lives studying coprolites. They can tell whether a dinosaur was a meat-eater or a plant-eater. If they find bones in a meat-eater's dung, they can work out what animals the meat-eater fed on.

Most of the fossil preparation takes place in the laboratory. Palaeontologists (scientists who study fossils) work with dental drills, ice picks, needles and paint brushes. They use these tools to chip away the final bits of rock around a fossil.

WHO'S THE BIGGEST?

For many years, scientists believed *Tyrannosaurus rex* was the largest meat-eating dinosaur. Then, in the mid 1990s, *Giganotosaurus* was discovered. Scientists believe this dinosaur may have been 13 to 14 metres long. Its skull measured 1.8 metres long. Then, in 2006, new research showed crocodile-jawed *Spinosaurus* was even bigger than *Giganotosaurus*, and *Spinosaurus* was up to 15 metres long. It had 1.8-metre-long spines on its back that formed a sail-like fin.

Spinosaurus

MESOZOIC ERA

Eoraptor

TRIASSIC PERIOD
251 to 200 million years ago
One of the world's first dinosaurs, *Eoraptor*, appears. There are also seed-bearing plants and mammals.

JURASSIC PERIOD
200 to 145 million years ago
Large and small dinosaurs and flying creatures evolve.

Triceratops

CRETACEOUS PERIOD
145 to 65 million years ago
Huge dinosaurs evolve, such as *Triceratops* and *T.rex*, but they become extinct at the end of this period.

CENOZOIC ERA

TERTIARY PERIOD
65 to 1.75 million years ago
Giant mammals and huge hunting birds appear. Our first human relatives start to evolve.

Smilodon

QUATERNARY PERIOD
1.75 million years ago to now
Time of ice ages and mammals, such as *Smilodon*. Modern humans, *Homo sapiens*, appear.

HOW COAL IS FORMED

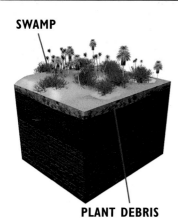

SWAMP

PLANT DEBRIS

About 300 million years ago, tree-filled swamps covered much of the earth. As trees and other plants died, they settled to the bottom of these swamps. There, this matter began to decay.

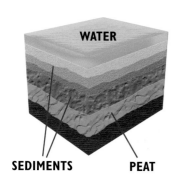

WATER

SEDIMENTS   PEAT

The decaying matter formed peat. This spongy material was soon buried under more layers.

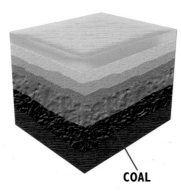

COAL

After millions of years of pressure and heat, the peat became coal.

FOSSIL FUELS

The remains of ancient plants and animals also turned into coal, oil and natural gas. These materials formed over 300 million years ago – before the time of the dinosaurs. This is why we call them fossil fuels.

During this period, the land was covered with swamps. The swamps were filled with huge trees, ferns and other large plants. Some plants grew up to 20 metres tall.

COAL, OIL AND GAS

Coal looks like a hard, black rock. It is actually the fossilised remains of large swamp plants that lived during the Carboniferous Period.

Oil and gas are also fossil fuels that formed during the Carboniferous Period. When tiny marine plants and animals called plankton died, they sank to the seabed. Here they were buried in clay and mud. Over millions of years, these sediments turned to rock. Heat and pressure underground made the layer of plankton turn to oil and gas.

These fuels took millions of years to form. We say they are a non-renewable resource. This means once they have been used up, they can never be replaced.

DRILLING FOR OIL

When a drill strikes oil, a thick, black liquid, called crude oil, comes gushing out of the ground. However, the petrol we put in our cars is usually a clear liquid. That's because the oil from the ground is taken to a refinery where it is separated into different liquids, called fractions. These liquids are then made into all sorts of products, such as crayons, textiles, plastics, jet fuel, fertilisers, heating oil and even cosmetics!

Oil reservoirs are
often found below the
sea. Oil rigs are built
on platforms to drill
the oil and gas and
pipe them ashore.
Some platforms float
on the sea while others
sit on legs that rest on
the seabed.

Today, coal miners use drills and computer-controlled machines to
remove coal from deep below the ground. Some underground mines are
over 1.5 kilometres deep. This image shows a control panel for a coal
mining operation.

FROM SHELLFISH TO CLIFFS

The oceans soak up the gas carbon dioxide from the atmosphere. Some of it is turned into carbonates (minerals that contain metals combined with carbon and oxygen). Animals such as oysters, mussels and clams use the carbonates to make their shells. When these shellfish die, their shells settle on the seabed. Over millions of years, the shells turn into sedimentary rock. The chalky white cliffs of Dover, in England, are made from the fossils of radiolaria. These tiny sea creatures measure just 0.001 millimetres across.

READING ROCKS

Every rock tells a story. Studying fossils in rocks is one of the best ways to see how the Earth's crust has moved around. For example, the fossils of sea animals have been found at the top of Mount Everest. This tells us that Mount Everest's rocks were formed under the ocean. Fossils in rocks can also tell us how plants and animals have changed. Over millions of years they have evolved into the wildlife we know today.

EXTINCTION

Fossils can also show us when and how sudden changes happened. For example, what caused the extinction of the dinosaurs around 65 million years ago? In the 1970s, scientists Luis and Walter Alvarez found very high levels

This artwork (below) shows the Chicxulub impact crater in Mexico soon after its creation. The crater is about 170 kilometres across. Scientists believe the crater was caused by an asteroid that measured 10 kilometres across. The impact would have caused devastation on Earth. Many scientists believe this event caused the extinction of the dinosaurs.

of the mineral iridium in some rocks. These rocks dated from the time of the end of the dinosaurs. Iridium is usually a sign of massive volcanic eruptions or a giant asteroid hitting Earth. Other rocks showed a white stripe where tonnes of seawater and rock may have been hurled into the air. This suggested to the scientists that Earth was hit by a giant asteroid. The asteroid wiped out the dinosaurs!

CLIMATE CHANGE

Studying ancient rocks helps scientists to understand what is happening to the Earth today. Looking back in time, they can see what happened the last time there was a big change in the Earth's climate. This might give us some clues as to what will happen in the next 100 years as our planet gets warmer.

A geologist studies crystals in the Cave of Crystals, Chihuahua, Mexico. The cave is 290 metres deep and contains some of the largest crystals in the world.

STUDYING ROCKS

GEOLOGISTS
Scientists who study rocks are called geologists. By looking at ancient rocks, geologists have worked out that the Earth is around 4.5 billion years old.

USING TECHNOLOGY
Creep meters are buried underground. They detect the movements of the Earth's tectonic plates. This helps scientists to predict earthquakes. Even if two plates move just the thickness of a human hair, a creep meter will pick it up.

ROBOT SCIENTISTS
Sometimes volcanoes are too hot or dangerous for scientists to approach. The Dante II robot (above) was used to explore Mount Spurr, a volcano in Alaska, USA. Dante II entered the volcano's crater. It collected gas and water samples, and recorded video images.

SPACE ROCKS
Scientists are keen to study rocks from other planets in our solar system. Mars Rover robots are collecting samples, such as rocks, from the surface of Mars. However, scientists are still working out how to get the samples back to Earth!

GLOSSARY

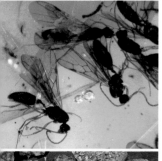

asteroid A jagged, rocky body. Most are found orbiting the Sun, between Mars and Jupiter in an area called the asteroid belt. Some asteroids can be nearly 1,000 kilometres across.

climate The average weather in an area over a long period of time.

coal A hard, black rock-like fossil fuel. Coal is the fossilised remains of large swamp plants that lived 300 million years ago in the Carboniferous Period.

crust The outer layer of the Earth. The crust is about 40 kilometres thick beneath the continental landmasses and seven kilometres thick beneath the oceans.

crystals Solid minerals whose molecules form patterns, that create regular shapes with angles and flat surfaces. Amethysts, diamonds and quartz are all crystals.

earthquake A violent shaking of the ground. It is caused by rocks cracking and breaking deep underground. This happens when they are put under stress due to movements of the Earth's tectonic plates.

erosion The process of material (such as rock fragments) being carried away by the movement of wind, water or ice.

extrusive rock Igneous rocks formed from lava that has erupted from volcanoes or been forced through cracks in the Earth's surface. The lava cools and hardens to form the rock. Extrusive rocks are also called volcanic rocks.

fault A crack in the Earth's crust.

fault mountains Mountains formed as a result of cracks in the Earth's surface along a fault line. Layers of rock on one side of the fault can be pushed up to form a mountain.

fold mountains Mountains formed when tectonic plates push against each other, fold and rise up. Mountains are pushed up at upfolds and valleys form in downfolds. The Andes Mountain chain and the Himalayan range are both examples of fold mountains.

fossils The remains of a once living thing, such as an animal or plant, preserved in rock.

fossil fuels Oil, natural gas and coal. They are called fossil fuels because they were made from the decaying remains of animals, plants and other organisms.

geology The study of the Earth, how it is made and how it evolved.

granite An intrusive igneous rock made up of the minerals, quartz, feldspar and mica. Many modern monuments are made of granite.

igneous rock Rock formed from magma that has reached the Earth's surface and cooled. To remember that igneous rocks are caused by great heat and fire, think of the word 'ignite'.

intrusive rock Igneous rocks such as granite. They are formed from magma that has cooled below the Earth's surface.

landmasses The large areas of land on which we live, such as North America and Europe.

lava Molten material made of rock, gas and other debris that comes from an erupting volcano. Before it reaches the surface, this material is known as magma.

limestone A sedimentary rock composed largely of the mineral calcite. Limestone was formed from the ancient remains of sea creatures such as shellfish.

lithosphere The hard outer layer of the Earth formed from the crust and the uppermost part of the mantle. On average, the lithosphere is about 100 kilometres deep. The word lithosphere comes from the Greek word 'lithos', which means 'stone'.

magma The fiery, flowing mix of rock found in the Earth's mantle and outer core. The heat and pressure inside the Earth keeps the material in this semi-fluid state. When magma manages to escape to the surface of the planet, it is called lava.

mantle The Earth's middle layer. The mantle has an average thickness of 2,900 kilometres.

marble A hard metamorphic rock that can be polished. It is often used for sculpture or as a building material.

metamorphic rock Rock that has been transformed from one type of rock into another. Most metamorphic rock forms because of great heat and pressure deep within the Earth. To remember this process think of the word 'morph', which means 'to change'.

microbes Living things that are so small they can only be seen with a microscope, such as bacteria.

minerals Solid, usually inorganic (non-living), substances that occur naturally on Earth. Gold, copper, iron and halite (table salt) are all minerals.

nitrates A group of chemical salts containing nitrogen. Nitrates occur naturally and are essential for plant growth.

ore A rock or mineral containing metal that can be extracted (removed). Ores are mined for the metals they contain.

pluton A giant lump of rock created when magma reservoirs harden underground.

porous A material that has really small spaces that air or water can pass through.

refinery A place where oil or metals are processed. An oil refinery turns crude oil into usable products such as fuel and plastics.

reservoir A place where liquids collect and are stored. Molten magma collects in natural reservoirs underground. People build reservoirs, such as lakes, to collect water.

sandstone A sedimentary rock made of mainly sand-sized grains of minerals and rocks. The grains have become naturally cemented together.

sediment Grains of materials such as rock and sand.

sedimentary rock Rock formed from layers of sediment. Over many years, pressure from the layers above and low heat packs the sediments together until they form new rock.

silt Tiny pieces of dirt in ponds, lakes and rivers. Silt is a type of sediment.

tectonic plates The giant jigsaw-like pieces of the Earth's lithosphere. The plates float on the Earth's mantle and are constantly moving at a very slow rate.

trinitite The shiny, green metamorphic rock formed from the intense heat and pressure of atomic testing in the Muerto Desert, USA in 1945.

volcano An opening in the Earth's crust through which gas, ash, and magma escape from the mantle. Volcanic eruptions can cause a mountain to form from lava that has cooled and hardened.

weathering The gradual breakdown of rock. Over time, wind, water and other surface factors wear away a rock's surface until it crumbles.